PowerKids Readers:

The Bilingual Library of the United States of America™

Bilingual Edition
English / Spanish
Edición bilingüe

RHODE ISLAND

JENNIFER WAY

TRADUCCIÓN AL ESPAÑOL: MARÍA CRISTINA BRUSCA

The Rosen Publishing Group's
PowerKids Press™ & **Editorial Buenas Letras**™
New York

Published in 2006 by The Rosen Publishing Group, Inc.
29 East 21st Street, New York, NY 10010

First Edition

Book Design: Albert B. Hanner
Photo Credits: Cover, p. 30 (state nickname) © Kelly-Mooney Photography/Corbis; p. 5, 25, 30 (State Motto) © Joseph Sohm; ChromoSohm Inc./Corbis; pp. 7, 31 (border) © 2002 Geoatlas; pp. 9, 31 (coastline) © David H. Wells; p. 11, 31 (Hopkins), (Hutchinson) © Bettmann/Corbis; pp. 13, 31 (temple) © Bob Krist/Corbis; p. 15, 17, 31 (Howe) © Corbis; p. 19 © Catherine Karnow/Corbis; p. 21 © Jeff Albertson/Corbis; p. 23 Providence Children's Museum, 100 South Street, Providence, RI 02903; p. 30 (state flower) © Frank Krahmer/zefa/Corbis, (state bird) © Robert Dowling/Corbis, (state tree) © W. Deuter/zefa/Corbis; pp. 31 (Stuart) © Stapleton Collection/Corbis, (Perry) © Medford Historical Society Collection/Corbis, (Lovecraft) Albert B. Hanner, (lighthouse) © Nick Wheeler/Corbis

Library of Congress Cataloging-in-Publication Data

Way, Jennifer.
  Rhode Island / Jennifer Way ; traducción al español, María Cristina Brusca. — 1st ed.
      p. cm. — (The bilingual library of the United States of America)
  Includes bibliographical references and index.
  ISBN 1-4042-3105-6 (library binding)
  1. Rhode Island—Juvenile literature. I. Title. II. Series.
  F79.3.W395 2006
  974.5-dc22
                                                            2005026283

Manufactured in the United States of America

Due to the changing nature of Internet links, Editorial Buenas Letras has developed an online list of Web sites related to the subject of this book. This site is updated regularly. Please use this link to access the list:

http://www.buenasletraslinks.com/ls/rhodeisland

Contents

Contenido

Welcome to Rhode Island

Rhode Island is the smallest state in the United States. Its official name is Rhode Island and Providence Plantations. The state motto is Hope.

Bienvenidos a Rhode Island

Rhode Island es el estado más pequeño de los Estados Unidos. Su nombre oficial es *Rhode Island and Providence Plantations*. El lema del estado es Esperanza.

Rhode Island Flag and State Seal

Bandera y escudo de Rhode Island

Rhode Island Geography

Rhode Island is one of six states in an area known as New England. Rhode Island shares a border with Connecticut and Massachusetts. Rhode Island also borders on the Atlantic Ocean.

Geografía de Rhode Island

Rhode Island es uno de seis estados en la región conocida como Nueva Inglaterra. Rhode Island linda con Connecticut y Massachusetts. También linda con el océano Atlántico.

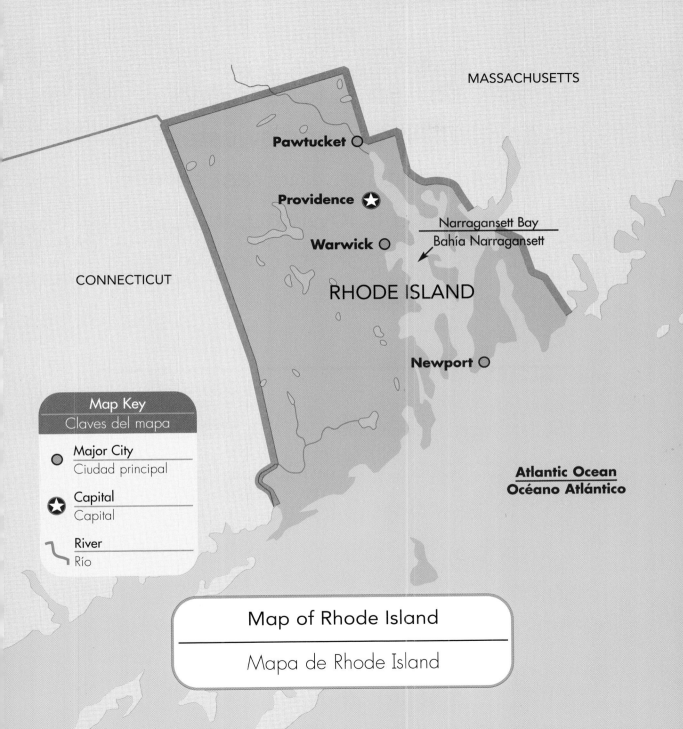

MASSACHUSETTS

Pawtucket ○

Providence ⭐

Warwick ○

Narragansett Bay
Bahía Narragansett

RHODE ISLAND

CONNECTICUT

Newport ○

Atlantic Ocean
Océano Atlántico

Map Key
Claves del mapa

○ Major City
   Ciudad principal

⭐ Capital
   Capital

〰 River
   Río

Map of Rhode Island

Mapa de Rhode Island

Rhode Island has forests and rolling hills in the northwestern area of the state. The rest of Rhode Island is lowland, with beaches, salt ponds, coastline, and fewer trees.

La región noroeste de Rhode Island tiene bosques y colinas. El resto de Rhode Island está formado por tierras bajas y costas con lagunas saladas, playas y pocos árboles.

Narragansett Bay

Bahía Narragansett

Rhode Island History

In 1636, Roger Williams and a group of followers settled in Narragansett Bay. Williams named the town Providence. This became the first English settlement in Rhode Island.

Historia de Rhode Island

En 1636, Roger Williams y un grupo de colonos se establecieron en Narragansett. Williams llamó a este pueblo Providence. Providence fue el primer establecimiento inglés de Rhode Island.

Roger Williams Arriving at Rhode Island

Llegada de Roger Williams a Rhode Island

Rhode Island was the first colony to allow freedom of religion. This means that people could practice any faith. People from many religions came to Rhode Island for this reason.

Rhode Island fue la primera colonia que permitió la libertad religiosa. Esto quiere decir que cada persona podía elegir y practicar su religión. Por esta razón, personas de muchas religiones diferentes se establecieron en Rhode Island.

Touro Synagogue in Newport, Rhode Island
The First Jewish temple in the United States

Sinagoga Touro en Newport, Rhode Island
Primer templo judío de los Estados Unidos

Nathanael Greene was a general in the American Revolution from 1775 until 1783. Greene led the Continental Army during many battles in the South. He was born in Potowomut, Rhode Island, in 1742.

Nathanael Greene fue un general de la Guerra de Independencia, de 1775 a 1783. Greene comandó el Ejército Continental en muchas batallas libradas en el sur. Greene nació en Potowomut, Rhode Island, en 1742.

Nathanael Greene

Ida Lewis was a famous Rhode Island lighthouse keeper. She lived from 1842 until 1911. Through the years, Ida Lewis saved at least 18 people from the waters surrounding the Lime Rock Lighthouse.

Ida Lewis fue una famosa farera de Rhode Island. Nació en 1842 y murió en 1911. Ida Lewis rescató a, por lo menos, 18 personas de las aguas que rodean el faro Lime Rock.

Ida Lewis

Living in Rhode Island

People from all over the world have made Rhode Island their home. Rhode Island has one of the oldest and largest Portuguese-American communities in the United States.

La vida en Rhode Island

Gente de todo el mundo ha encontrado su hogar en Rhode Island. Rhode Island tiene una de las más grandes y antiguas comunidades portuguesas de los Estados Unidos.

Portuguese Festival in Providence, Rhode Island

Festival portugués en Providence, Rhode Island

Rhode Island is known for its sailing and fishing. Every summer people come from all over to enjoy these activities. Rhode Island is called the Ocean State.

Rhode Island es conocido por la pesca y la navegación de vela. Cada verano, muchos turistas visitan el estado para disfrutar de estas actividades. Rhode Island es llamado el Estado Océano.

Boats Docked in Newport Harbor

Barcos atracados en la bahía Newport

The Providence Children's Museum is a fun place to visit. At the museum kids can play and learn about nature and history.

Es muy divertido visitar el Museo Infantil de Providence. En este museo los niños pueden jugar al tiempo que aprenden acerca de la naturaleza y la historia.

Dragon on the Providence Children's Museum

Dragón en el Museo Infantil de Providence

Providence, Warwick, Cranston, Newport, and Pawtucket are the biggest cities in Rhode Island. Providence is the capital of the state of Rhode Island.

Providence, Warwick, Cranston, Newport y Pawtucket son las ciudades más grandes de Rhode Island. Providence es la capital del estado de Rhode Island.

State Capitol in Providence, Rhode Island
___
Capitolio del estado en Providence, Rhode Island

Activity:
Let´s Draw the Rhode Island Flag

Actividad:
Dibujemos la bandera de Rhode Island

1

Draw a rectangle. Add the flag's border around the edge of the rectangle.

Dibuja un rectángulo. Agrega el borde de la bandera, alrededor del rectángulo.

2

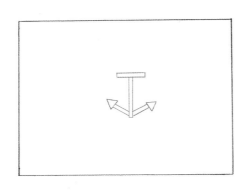

Draw an anchor in the center of the rectangle.

Dibuja un ancla en el centro del rectángulo.

3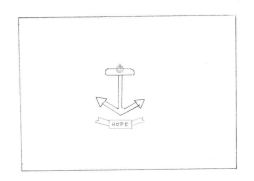

Draw a ribbon under the anchor. Write the word "HOPE" on the ribbon.

Dibuja una cinta debajo del ancla. Escribe en la cinta la palabra "HOPE".

4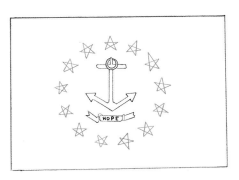

Draw 13 stars around the anchor. Make changes to the ribbon as shown.

Dibuja 13 estrellas alrededor del ancla. Modifica la cinta, como en la muestra.

5

Color in your flag.

Colorea tu bandera.

Timeline

Cronología

Dutch explorer Adriaen Block visits the island now named for him.	**1614**	El explorador holandés Adriaen Block visita la isla que ahora lleva su nombre.
Roger Williams founds Providence, the first permanent British settlement in Rhode Island.	**1636**	Roger Williams funda Providence, el primer establecimiento inglés de Rhode Island.
Rhode Island colonists burn the British ship Gaspée to protest British taxes.	**1772**	Los colonos de Rhode Island queman el barco británico Gaspée en protesta por los impuestos británicos.
Rhode Island is the first of the thirteen colonies to declare its independence from Britain.	**1778**	Rhode Island es la primera de las trece colonias en declararse independiente de Gran Bretaña.
Rhode Island becomes the 13th state.	**1790**	Rhode Island se convierte en el estado 13.
The first America's Cup yacht race is held in Newport.	**1930**	Se realiza en Newport la primera regata Copa América.
Newport Bridge is completed, linking Jamestown and Newport.	**1969**	Se completa el puente Newport que une Jameston y Newport.

Rhode Island Events

Eventos en Rhode Island

February
Newport Winter Festival, Newport

May
Scottish Highland Festival, Richmond

June
Narragansett Art Festival,
Narragansett
Newport International Film Festival,
Newport
International Polo Series, Portsmouth

July
Newport Music Festival, Newport
Newport Regatta, Newport
Portuguese Cultural Festival, Newport

August
Seafood Festival, Charlestown
Newport Jazz Festival, Newport
Greek Festival, Pawtucket

September
Newport International Boat Show,
Newport

October
Festa Italiana, Newport County

Febrero
Festival de invierno de Newport

Mayo
Festival escocés de las tierras altas,
en Richmond

Junio
Festival de las Artes de Narragansett,
en Narragansett
Festival internacional de cine de Newport
Torneo internacional de polo,
en Portsmouth

Julio
Festival de música de Newport
Regata Newport, en Newport
Festival de la cultura portuguesa, en Newport

Agosto
Festival de los mariscos, en Charlestown
Festival de jazz de Newport
Festival griego, en Pawtucket

Septiembre
Exposición internacional de barcos,
en Newport

Octubre
Fiesta italiana, en el condado Newport

Rhode Island Facts/
Datos sobre Rhode Island

Population
1 milllion

Población
1 millón

Capital
Providence

Capital
Providence

State Motto
Hope

Lema del estado
Esperanza

State Flower
Violet

Flor del estado
Violeta

State Bird
Rhode Island Red

Ave del estado
Gallina roja de
Rhode Island

State Nickname
The Ocean State

Mote del estado
El Estado Océano

State Tree
Red Maple

Árbol del estado
Arce rojo

State Song
"Rhode Island's It for Me"

Canción del estado
"Rhode Island para mí"

Famous Rhode Islanders/ Rodislandeses famosos

Anne Hutchinson
(1591–1643)

Settler
Colona

Esek Hopkins
(1718–1802)

American revolutionary
Revolucionario

Gilbert Stuart
(1755–1828)

Artist
Artista

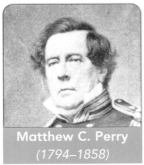

Matthew C. Perry
(1794–1858)

Naval officer
Oficial naval

Julia Ward Howe
(1819–1910)

Author
Escritora

H. P. Lovecraft
(1890–1937)

Author
Escritor

Words to Know/Palabras que debes saber

border
frontera

coastline
terrenos costeros

lighthouse
faro

temple
templo

Here are more books to read about Rhode Island:
Otros libros que puedes leer acerca de Rhode Island:

In English/En inglés:

R is for Rhode Island Red:
A Rhode Island Alphabet
by Allio, Mark R.
Sleeping Bear Press, 2005

Rhode Island
by Heinrichs, Ann
Child's World, 2005

Words in English: 320   Palabras en español: 332

Index

Índice